THE QUESTION FIRST GROUP

The 4 Pillars of Breakthrough Sales Communication

The Pathfinder's Way

First published by The Question First Group LLC 2025

Copyright © 2025 by The Question First Group

All rights reserved. No part of this publication may be reproduced, stored or transmitted in any form or by any means, electronic, mechanical, photocopying, recording, scanning, or otherwise without written permission from the publisher. It is illegal to copy this book, post it to a website, or distribute it by any other means without permission.

The Question First Group has no responsibility for the persistence or accuracy of URLs for external or third-party Internet Websites referred to in this publication and does not guarantee that any content on such Websites is, or will remain, accurate or appropriate.

The Four Pillars of Breakthrough Sales Communication (Yes, And; Vanguarding; Question First; The Law of Three), The Pathfinder's Compass, the associated frameworks, names, and all original illustrations, graphics, and tools contained in this work are proprietary intellectual property of The Question First Group LLC and are protected under United States copyright and trademark law.

Unauthorized use, reproduction, or distribution of these concepts, names, or illustrations is strictly prohibited.

Fair Use Notice

Brief quotations and references from this book may be used for purposes of review, commentary, teaching, or research, provided that proper attribution is given to The 4 Pillars of Breakthrough Sales Communication: The Pathfinder's Way by The Question First Group LLC. Any other reproduction, adaptation, or distribution of the proprietary frameworks, names, or illustrations requires prior written permission from the publisher.

First edition

ISBN (print): 979-8-9930272-0-3
ISBN (digital): 979-8-9930272-3-4

Cover art by Pixels Ink
Illustration by Pixels Ink

This book was professionally typeset on Reedsy.
Find out more at reedsy.com

Contents

Introduction	1

I Why Sales Conversations Are Broken (and How to Fix Them)

1	It All Starts with…Discovery	7
2	The Death of Sales Training	9
3	How the Breakthrough Communication System is Different	12
4	A Word Before We Begin	14

II The Four Pillars: A Pathfinder's Essential Tools

5	The Core Pillars of Breakthrough Communication	19
6	Pillar I: Yes, And - The Force That Drives Momentum	23
7	Pillar II: Vanguarding - Eliminating Objections Before They…	28
8	Pillar III: Question First - Stop Pitching, Start Guiding	34
9	Pillar IV: The Law of Three - Digging Deeper in Every…	39

III The I³ Discovery Framework

10 I³: The Roadmap to Success 45

IV The Pathfinder's Compass

11 Your Transformation: Becoming a Pathfinder 51

V Your Breakthrough Journey Starts Now

12 What Now? 61
13 A Personal Story: The Power of Transformation 65

Notes 67
About the Author 68
Also by The Question First Group 70

Introduction

Trust and Connection.

They are *not* soft skills.

They are the core currencies of sales.

Everything—and I really do mean *everything*—in business depends on how quickly and deeply you earn them.

Those who master this win fast and win big.

Those who don't? They grind. They chase. And they're left wondering...Why did they not buy?

What you're about to read isn't just a framework. It's a system.

And when applied, it works—extraordinarily well.

If you're ready to stop guessing and start communicating in a way that creates instant *resonance and connection* with buyers...

If you're ready to go beyond surface-level conversations and build the kind of trust that closes deals and keeps clients for life...

Then let's get into it.

Here's why this matters more than ever...

Think back to the last time a salesperson truly *got* you. Not just your surface-level needs, but your deeper motivations—what actually drove your decision.

That conversation didn't feel like a pitch. It wasn't a checklist. It was a real dialogue—one that left you feeling understood, guided, and confident in your next step.

In other words, a *connection* was made.

Now, be honest: how often do you experience that type of connection as a buyer today?

How often do you say, "My goodness. That salesperson was extraordinary. They get me. They get us. Wow."

You're likely thinking: Rarely, if ever.

Now, how about *your* organization's sales team?

Are they making deep, unforgettable connections with the prospects they're meeting with every day, or are they leaving most of your potential customers to feel exactly as you feel during those empty interactions?

Here's the reality: Most sales conversations today are mechanical. Scripted. Transactional. Salespeople ask *what* you need, but rarely *why* it matters. They check boxes instead of digging deep.

The result? Shallow conversations. Weak connections. Lost deals.

At its core, selling isn't about pushing products or reading from a script. It's about creating a connection so strong that buyers see *and* feel the value in both you and your solution.

But when sales becomes all about processes, automation, and metrics, the human side disappears. Trust erodes. And when buyers don't trust, they don't buy.

Somewhere along the way, we took the *soul* out of sales.

This needs to change...and at The Question First Group[1], our obsession is bringing the true art of "deep connection" back to sales.

Difficult?

Yes.

Possible?

Absolutely.

In fact, we're seeing it every day.

I

Why Sales Conversations Are Broken (and How to Fix Them)

Sales today isn't broken because of a lack of tools or technology. It's broken because most conversations are shallow, scripted, and disconnected from what buyers truly need.

In this section, we'll uncover why discovery has gone missing, why training fails, and why old systems can't keep up. Only by seeing what's broken can we prepare to fix it—and open the door to a new way forward.

1

It All Starts with...Discovery

What's the heart of the problem?

59% of business buyers say most sales reps don't take the time to understand them, and 73% of buyers say most sales interactions feel transactional (Salesforce[2]).

Most reps identify a problem but never dig into its real impact. They jump to solutions without truly understanding the buyer's world.

Poor discovery is the biggest barrier to closing deals.

Why? Because we're focused on the wrong things.

We've prioritized the *Science of Selling*—processes, scripts, technology, and efficiency—while abandoning the *Art of Selling*.

And that's the mistake.

Great salespeople don't just sell. They guide. They uncover. They help buyers see their challenges clearly *before* offering a solution.

Miss that step, and you've likely lost the deal.

2

The Death of Sales Training

But this unique ability to connect deeply through powerful discovery doesn't happen by itself.

We all know connection, discovery, and the ability to ask effective questions are essential to sales. We also know that very, very few do it incredibly well.

The core problem here isn't knowled**ge**. It's application.

And the reason we have such a dearth of application? Sales training is all but non-existent today.

Sure, we have sales "meetings." But trainings? No. Not at all.

What makes for world-class sales training? Two words: "Role Plays"

Don't roll your eyes here—that's what most leaders, managers, and sales professionals do when they hear "role play." They act as if such training is beneath them.

What a tragedy.

From years of observing and training sales teams, we've found that fewer than 2% consistently role-play each week.

This leads to a mind-boggling problem:

We're practicing sales on our customers instead of practicing on ourselves.

You're literally PRACTICING SELLING on your potential customers.

If that doesn't bother you, nothing will.

Most organizations are losing millions annually because they aren't doing what it takes to build an extraordinary culture of sales training.

For massive change in your organization's sales results, three things must occur:

1. **Leadership must become obsessed** with creating an extraordinary sales culture—and be willing to do what's necessary to get there.
2. **You must get serious about ongoing, weekly sales training** with "real" role plays. Sales leaders must shift from simply being "managers" to sales "trainers"—who also manage.

3. **You must instill an actual SYSTEM of communication** within your organization that everyone can follow—sales team, leaders, all team members, and certainly everyone customer-facing.

This book focuses on #3, something we've uniquely developed at The Question First Group.

#1 and #2 are about mindset and commitment—qualities that are the biggest difference between "average" and "extraordinary" sales cultures.

3

How the Breakthrough Communication System is Different

What makes our system unique is this: Unlike common sales systems today—Sandler, Baseline, Bant, Challenger—it doesn't *only* apply to your sales department.

Think about it: Would you rather have a system of effective communication that only your sales team follows, leaving the rest of the organization in the dark? Or one that literally *every single person* in your entire organization follows, learns from, and uses to create deeper connections?

We'll spend 95% of our time focused on *sales* in this book, but the application extends far beyond. Consider how these principles apply to other departments in your organization—and your personal life.

After all, the principles of great communication aren't specific to sales or business.

They're human.

And what's more human than communicating in a way that creates connection and breakthrough experiences?

That's the power of the Breakthrough Communication System.

4

A Word Before We Begin

One last thing before we dive into the Four Pillars.

In our experience, people approach new communication frameworks in one of two ways.

The first group reads with true curiosity: *"I recognize some of this, but I can see how applying this could make me so much better. This is going to require practice, but the results will be worth it."*

The second group reads with skepticism: *"This might work for others, but my industry is different. My sales process is unique. My customers are unlike anyone else's."*

Here's what we've learned after working with thousands of professionals across dozens of industries: The principles of human connection are universal. Whether you're selling software or boats, leading a team or raising a family, the fundamentals of breakthrough communication remain the same.

The specific tactics change. The underlying principles do not.

We're not asking you to abandon what makes your industry unique. We're asking you to apply these human communication principles within your expertise.

If you're willing to approach this with genuine curiosity—to test these concepts in your world and see what happens—you'll likely be surprised by the results.

Our commitment: We'll give you direct, actionable frameworks based on real-world experience.

Your commitment: Approach this with an open mind and a willingness to practice.

Sound fair?

II

The Four Pillars: A Pathfinder's Essential Tools

The Four Pillars drive breakthrough moments in every conversation. When used with intent and a genuine desire to help, they transform interactions from transactional to transformational.

Each pillar has a distinct role. We'll break them down with key concepts, real-world examples, and practical applications you can use immediately.

5

The Core Pillars of Breakthrough Communication

The *Four Pillars of Breakthrough Communication* transform how you connect, discover, and build trust. When mastered, they shift conversations from transactional to transformational.

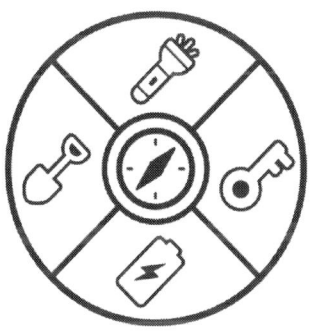

The Four Pillars of Breakthrough Communication

Each pillar serves a specific purpose:

Pillar I: Yes, And *(Battery)* – The practice of receiving any energy or situation—good, bad, or ugly—and transforming it into forward momentum that builds rather than derails progress.

Pillar II: Vanguarding *(Flashlight)* – The practice of foreseeing what could go wrong, being hyper-aware of potential concerns, and resolving them upfront to prevent disengagement, failure or distraction.

Pillar III: Question First *(Key)* – The practice of thinking, responding, and teaching through questions, creating moments of clarity, ownership, and transformation for others.

Pillar IV: The Law of Three *(Shovel)* – The practice of breaking through surface-level responses, knowing that real understanding is achieved only by asking successive, thoughtful questions creating transformative moments of clarity and self-discovery.

When your team masters these pillars, they stop being just sellers—they become **trusted guides**. Deals close with stronger commitment, and relationships deepen.

What You'll Learn

Beyond the Four Pillars, you'll discover:

The I^3 Discovery Framework – Issue, Impact, Importance. A simple roadmap that *any* sales professional can follow to ensure deep buyer discovery every time, preventing deals from stalling due to competing priorities.

The Pathfinder's Compass – Four communication styles that shape every interaction:

- **The Dictator** (command & control [without curiosity])
- **The Lawyer** (manipulative questioning)
- **The Instructor** (helpful but directive)
- **The Pathfinder** (genuinely curious, others-focused)

Your goal? Become a Pathfinder—the ultimate in transformational communication.

We'll break down each concept with real examples, common mistakes to avoid, and practical exercises you can implement immediately.

A System, Not Just Sales Techniques

Here's what makes this different: These aren't just sales tactics. They're human communication principles that work in leadership, parenting, and any relationship where connection matters.

Master these pillars, and you don't just improve your sales results—you transform how you influence, lead, and connect with everyone around you.

Author's Note:

This mini-book provides a comprehensive overview of the Break-

through Communication System. While it doesn't cover every nuance we teach in our full training, it will quickly reveal whether this is the communication framework you've been searching for. Visit <u>questionsfirstgroup.com</u>[3] to find out more about our sales workshops, coaching and training.

6

Pillar I: Yes, And - The Force That Drives Momentum

Build, Don't Break

The Problems This Solves:

- "Our team gets defensive when buyers point out what we lack."
- "When objections come up, we panic and start pitching."
- "We struggle to keep conversations focused on real pain points."
- "Our sales calls lack the right energy."
- "We just get 'stuck' a lot and I don't know why."

The Concept

Yes, And comes from improv, where actors must "go with" whatever they're given and build forward. In improv, this creates seamless performances. In communication, it creates breakthrough conversations.

Yes, And is the energy that moves conversations forward. It's not just avoiding "yeah, but" or "no"—it's a mindset that ensures progress, keeps dialogue constructive, and builds powerful momentum.

At its core, Yes, And:

- Builds on ideas instead of shutting them down
- Maintains momentum, even through objections
- Acknowledges concerns while staying on track
- Keeps focus on solutions without dismissing challenges
- Makes everyone feel heard, understood, and valued

Mastering the Flinch Moment

When caught off guard, most salespeople flinch—hesitate, stumble, or look uncomfortable. Buyers notice, and this erodes confidence instantly.

Yes, And eliminates the flinch. Instead of reacting with defensiveness or uncertainty, you meet objections with calm confidence. Your posture, tone, and body language should say: *I've got this* or *I was hoping you might ask that.*

If your sales team truly understands Yes, And, they will NEVER flinch again on a sales call.

That's how transformational this pillar is.

The Power of Nonverbal Energy

When you understand that Yes, And is all about energy, you become acutely aware of your nonverbal communication.

Studies show 93% of communication impact is nonverbal (Mehrabian[4]), yet nonverbal sales training is practically non-existent.

Here's the reality: ALL body language will be interpreted by the prospect. And all body language affects the energy of the moment.

Your team must master eye contact, nodding, and leaning in to show engagement—because energy is everything.

Yes, And in Action

Example 1: Handling Objections

Buyer: "Your system doesn't handle X, and that's a dealbreaker."

- **Weak Response:** "Yeah, but we have other features..." *(Defensive, dismissive)*
- **Yes, And Response:** "Good point. X is a challenge. Let's look at how we can still solve your biggest issue..." *(Acknowledges, redirects, builds momentum)*

Example 2: The Feature Dump Trap

Buyer: "Does your product integrate with every CRM?"

- **Weak Response:** "Well, we integrate with…" *(Feature dump begins)*
- **Yes, And Response:** "Great question! We integrate with most. But first, let's clarify exactly what you're trying to achieve so we can make sure the integration actually serves your needs."

You acknowledge the question but steer focus back to what matters.

Example 3: Flipping Concerns Into Strengths

Buyer: "I like what I'm hearing, but you don't have many reviews."

- **Weak Response:** "Uh, yeah, we're just getting going, that's why…"
- **Yes, And Response:** "Totally understand. And that's exactly why you're our most important customer—we'll ensure your experience sets the gold standard for future reviews."

Instead of defending, you turn the concern into an advantage.

Why Yes, And Works

- **Acknowledges without losing focus** – Buyers feel heard, but you stay in control
- **Guides discovery** – Keeps conversations centered on real pain points
- **Prevents feature dumps** – Keeps solutions tailored to actual needs
- **Maintains proper energy** – Creates the right energy at the right moment

Yes, And vs. Traditional Techniques

Traditional approaches like Active Listening ("So, what I hear you saying is...") and Mirroring can feel forced when overused.

Yes, And is different. It doesn't just reflect back—it builds forward.

Buyer: "We've been burned by bad software before."

- **Weak Response:** "I hear you. That sounds frustrating." *(Acknowledges but doesn't move forward)*
- **Yes, And Response:** "I hear you. And that's exactly why I want to make sure we get this right for you. Let's break down what went wrong last time so we can avoid it."

Yes, And isn't about *sounding* engaged—it's about leading conversations toward obvious next actions.

And that's what wins deals.

7

Pillar II: Vanguarding - Eliminating Objections Before They Arise

Proactively Prevent Predictable Problems

The Problems This Solves:

- "We're not setting the right tone for our sales meetings."
- "Surprise objections keep popping up during closing, stalling deals."
- "We often don't hear back from prospects we thought were ready to move forward."
- "Our prospects simply aren't opening up and being honest with us."

The Concept

The essence of Vanguarding is this: The greatest way to resolve a concern is to address it BEFORE it becomes a concern.

Buyers hesitate because of unspoken concerns. If we wait for them to surface (reactive), they derail momentum. Instead, we call them out first (proactive), closing the exit doors before they're used.

Example: Instead of waiting for price objections, you say: *"You might be thinking this price seems high. Let's break down why companies invest at this level and the ROI they see."*

By naming the concern first, you control the narrative, build trust, and keep the conversation moving.

Preparation: The Key to Vanguarding

Objections shouldn't surprise you. Before any sales call, ask yourself:

- What concerns are likely to come up?
- Where might the buyer hesitate?
- What's the biggest "but" that could stall this deal?
- What do we need to get in front of now to ensure progress later?

Taking just a few minutes to anticipate these objections ensures you stay ahead of them. Once identified, you can build your presentation to "vanguard" each concern.

Why Vanguarding Works:

- **Prevents stalls** – Removes friction before it slows progress
- **Projects confidence** – Shows buyers you understand their concerns

- **Sets the tone** – Creates a sense of order and expectations
- **Keeps you in control** – Avoids defensive scrambling when objections arise

Yes, And moves the conversation forward. Vanguarding clears the road ahead. Master both, and you stay in command of every conversation.

Vanguarding in Action

1. The Perfect Agenda

Most sales meetings lack clear direction, confusing prospects and killing deals. Less than 10% of sales professionals give a clear agenda at the start of their calls.

The Vanguard: *"The purpose of our conversation today is three-fold. First, we're going to identify the right windows and doors for your remodel. Second, I'll give you a quote with all options while I'm here. Third, assuming the quote fits your budget and you'd like to move forward, we'll secure your installation date with a deposit. Does that align with your expectations?"*

Now the prospect understands exactly what will happen and what "success" looks like.

Is your sales team this explicit when discussing agenda on their sales calls?

2. The Honest Agreement

Prospects often aren't honest because they don't want to hurt your feelings. Instead of hurting feelings, they lie—or hold back the truth. Vanguard this issue upfront.

The five steps:

1. State the importance of the conversation
2. Commit to being fully transparent, getting their confirmation
3. Let them know you'll ask questions they've likely never heard before
4. Tell them they will NOT hurt your feelings
5. Have them verbally commit to being open and honest

Example: *"Before we dive into your company's biggest needs, Jeff, I want to address something important. This decision will affect your organization for years to come. Because the stakes are high, we can't make mistakes. The key is our openness with each other. My promise: I'll be fully transparent with anything we discuss. That's what you deserve, fair? (yes) At the same time, I'll need to ask thoughtful questions you've likely never heard before. It's critical you're open and honest too. If there's anything you don't like, what do you need to say? (I need to tell you how I feel) Exactly! Will you commit to being open and honest about everything we discuss today?"*

When applied correctly, this is MAGICAL. It invites perfect energy and removes barriers that prevent honest communication. Can you imagine the potential impact this could have, assuming it was applied correctly, with your sales team?

Yes, it's awkward at first—because it's different. But remember: By making this verbal agreement early, you're much more likely to get a written agreement later.

3. Handling Price Objections Proactively

"I know price is an important factor, and we'll get there soon. First, let's make sure we fully understand your challenges so we can find the right solution."

You've acknowledged their concern without losing control of the conversation.

4. Addressing Implementation Concerns

"I know implementing new solutions can raise concerns. Before we dive in, tell me about your last rollout—what worked well, and what didn't?"

Now they share concerns on your terms, allowing you to guide the discussion.

Why Missed Vanguards Cost You Deals

Most stalled or lost conversations happen because a Vanguard was missed. When you fail to preempt an objection, the buyer fixates on it, derailing the call.

Vanguarding eliminates landmines before they explode. It builds confidence, keeps conversations moving, and ensures you stay in control from start to finish.

Again, it's critical to understand this key here: Almost all miscommunication and mishaps in sales could have been prevented with the proper vanguard.

So when things go wrong, always start with the simple question, "What vanguard did we miss?"

8

Pillar III: Question First - Stop Pitching, Start Guiding

Ask, Don't Tell

The Problems This Solves:

- "We keep explaining features, but buyers aren't pulling the trigger."
- "We talk way too much on our calls."
- "We don't see the engagement from prospects we should."
- "When buyers object, our team backpedals and defends."

The Concept

Most salespeople default to talking—pitching products, answering questions, and assuming they understand the buyer's problem. That's exactly why buyers resist.

Your job isn't to push solutions; it's to guide buyers to uncover their own solutions.

When buyers discover insights themselves, they **own** the idea. And ideas buyers own lead to commitment.

The Question First approach means asking intentional, deep questions that force buyers to confront their true problems and discover their own needs.

Deep Questions Drive Deep Connections

Consider a boat dealer using Question First mindset. Instead of pitching features, they ask questions few peers would ever consider:

- *"What's the most memorable experience you've had on the water, and how do you envision your next boat enhancing that?"*
- *"Tell me, what made you want to own a new boat at this point in your life?"*
- *"What role do you see this boat playing in your life over the next five to ten years?"*
- *"When you think about the perfect day on the water, who are you with and what are you doing?"*
- *"What's the biggest frustration you've had with previous boats, and how would you like to avoid that this time?"*

Notice how thoughtful and deep each question is? We've trained various marine dealerships, and the average salesperson asks NONE of these questions.

But when they do, the impact is extraordinary. Such questions encourage reflection, spark deeper thinking, and reveal what truly matters.

Is YOUR team asking discovery questions with this depth and quality?

When to Use Question First

1. **During Resistance:** Don't defend or pitch harder. Instead, clarify: *"Tell me more about why that's a concern for you."*
2. **Discovery Conversations:** Go deeper instead of accepting surface-level issues: *"What specific impact is that having on your business?"*
3. **When Suggesting Change:** People don't want to change... unless it's their idea: *"What would have to change to make that possible?"*

The 3Ps of a Perfect Question

Ever ask a question and get a frustrating look? There's a framework for asking the perfect question every time: **Progress, Purpose, Path.**

- **Progress:** Your question should always move the conversation forward
- **Purpose:** Buyers must clearly see why you're asking
- **Path:** Questions must be simple enough for buyers to "find" the answer without confusion

Breaking Down the 3Ps

Progress: Move the conversation forward

If someone says *"Where are you going with this?"* or *"I already told you..."* your question lacked progress.

- **Weak:** *"What do you think of our product?"* (too vague, no clear direction)
- **Stronger:** *"When you look at our product, what feature would have the biggest impact on your business?"* (clearly moves toward identifying needs)

Purpose: They must feel the "Why"

When questions lack purpose, you'll hear *"Why are you asking that?"* or *"What's your point?"*

- **Weak:** *"What do you think about this project?"* (unclear purpose)
- **Stronger:** *"Do you see any hidden roadblocks in this project we haven't discussed yet?"* (clearly identifies risks)

Path: Give them a clear route to the answer

Without a clear path, you'll get blank looks or hear *"I'm confused by your question."*

- **Weak:** *"What's your company's biggest challenge right now?"* (too vague)
- **Stronger:** *"What's your company's biggest marketing challenge right now?"*

Notice how adding one word (marketing) creates a much clearer path to the answer.

3Ps in Action

Buyer: "I'm worried your product won't integrate well with our system."

- **Weak Response:** "Our product integrates seamlessly with everything." (defensive pitch)
- **Question First Response:** "Can you tell me more specifically about your concerns with integration?"

This incorporates all three Ps:

- **Progress:** Moves directly toward resolving the objection
- **Purpose:** Clearly addresses the buyer's concern
- **Path:** Makes it easy for them to elaborate thoughtfully

Although the 3Ps are challenging to master, once your team learns to apply them consistently, buyers will stop seeing them as "just another sales rep" and instead see them as a trusted advisor helping them uncover real solutions.

Stop selling. Start asking.

Great questions create clarity. Clarity creates commitment.

9

Pillar IV: The Law of Three - Digging Deeper in Every Conversation

To Get To Core, Ask More

The Problems This Solves:

- "Our sales team isn't going beyond the surface with their conversations."
- "We're not uncovering our buyers' real challenges."
- "Our discovery calls feel rushed or shallow."
- "We're finding out late in the process there were other concerns we hadn't identified."
- "We're simply not connecting with the prospect at the level we need to achieve."

The Concept

To get to the core of any issue, you generally have to ask three or more questions along the same vein.

Once you start thinking with a Question First mindset, the next essential pillar is The Law of Three, rooted in this truth: the first answer is never the full story.

If you stop asking questions too soon, you're operating on assumptions—and assumptions kill deals. Most sales professionals never go beyond surface-level questions because they haven't been trained to truly dig deeper.

How Do You Know You've Hit the Core?

There are three key indicators you've reached the real issue:

1. **The "Aha" or "Lightbulb" Moment** The buyer hits clarity—*"Wow, I never realized that's the real issue..."* When buyers experience their own breakthroughs, they're more committed to action because it was *their* idea.
2. **Emotional Understanding** You uncover deeper emotional drivers—how the problem affects them personally, their team, or their business. This reveals the true urgency behind their concern.
3. **A Clear, Concrete Picture** You reach clarity where both you and the buyer can visualize the problem or path forward. If you can't paint this picture, you're not done asking questions.

Remember: It might take three questions, or it might take ten. The point is to go deep until one (if not all) of these outcomes emerges.

The Law of Three in Action

- **Buyer:** *"Our current software isn't flexible enough."*
- **Weak Response:** "Good to know!" *(then immediately pitches a solution)*

Law of Three Response:

- **Follow-up 1:** *"How is that impacting your daily operations?"*
- **Follow-up 2:** *"What effect is that having on your team's productivity?"*
- **Follow-up 3:** *"What happens to the business if this issue isn't fixed soon?"*
- **Follow-up 4:** *"And on an emotional level for you as a CEO, what type of effect has this had on you personally?"*

Instead of pitching prematurely, you've uncovered how the issue directly impacts revenue, productivity, and team morale. Now your solution speaks to the real pain—not a superficial symptom.

The Power of Going Deep

When your team masters deeper questioning, they'll hear these statements constantly from prospects:

1. *"I don't know why I'm telling you this, but I feel like I can trust you."*
2. *"No one has ever asked me that before…wow."*
3. *"Come to think of it, now I think I realize the real problem…"*
4. *"I've only known you for five minutes but I feel like I can tell*

you this..."

These responses signal breakthrough moments—when prospects move from guarded to open, from surface-level to deep truth.

The Bottom Line

The first answer is rarely the real answer.

Most salespeople accept the initial response and jump to solutions. But the real gold lies deeper. When you consistently apply The Law of Three, you'll uncover the true drivers behind every decision.

Ask deeper questions. Get better answers. Make extraordinary connections. And close bigger deals.

III

The I³ Discovery Framework

Now that you understand the Four Pillars of breakthrough communication, your team needs a proven structure to guide your discovery conversations. This is where I³ comes in.

While hundreds of sales frameworks exist—Sandler, Challenger, BANT—most miss a critical element. At The Question First Group, we've found the most effective discovery system is I³: Issue, Impact, Importance.

10

I³: The Roadmap to Success

Created by Ian Altman (author of *Same-Side Selling*[5] and mentor to Marcus Sheridan), I³ provides a clear roadmap that uncovers the most critical information needed to move forward—or not—with any sale.

Here's how it works, and why the order matters:

Issue: Understanding the Pain

Issue is about understanding the prospect's pain. What problem (or problems) are they trying to solve?

The key here is using The Law of Three to discover the "why" behind each issue. Don't just identify the problem—understand what's driving it.

Critical Mistake to Avoid: Don't move to "Impact" until ALL issues have been brought to light. This is where most sales professionals rush the process and miss crucial problems.

Impact: Quantifying the Cost

Once you've defined the problems, dig into the **effect** these issues are having on the organization—both individually and collectively.

Your goal is to draw out:

- **Financial impact** - What is this costing the company?
- **Emotional impact** - How is this affecting people personally?
- **Operational impact** - What's the broader effect on the business?

The Law of Three is essential here. Done correctly, you'll know exactly what the problem is costing the prospect—financially, emotionally, operationally, and personally.

All of it matters.

Key Practice: At the end of Impact, always ask the prospect to summarize in 2-3 sentences the impact of their issues. Then, once they've done this, confirm what they've just stated by repeating it as well. Doing this creates a very concrete "impact" statement that can be called back again and again, as needed.

Importance: The Deal-Maker or Deal-Breaker

Here's where most sales systems fail, and why deals mysteriously stall:

"I just don't get it. We defined the need. We discussed the impact.

They agreed they want to solve the problem...yet they've gone silent. Why?"

The answer? They skipped Importance.

Importance determines whether solving this problem ranks higher than the competing priorities the company faces.

Just because your prospect has a problem and knows what it's costing them doesn't mean your solution is their most important priority right now.

The Reality: Unless the issue you solve is in the buyer's "Top 3" needs, you likely won't make the cut, and the sale will stall.

Your Job: Don't simply accept their list of priorities as given. Often, prospects haven't fully thought through what should be solved first. Help them clarify what truly deserves immediate attention.

Why I³ Works

The Four Pillars give you the communication skills. I³ gives you the roadmap. Together, they ensure you never miss critical information, never waste time on low-priority prospects, and always know exactly where you stand in the buying process.

When you master both the Pillars and I³, discovery becomes predictable, powerful, and profitable.

IV

The Pathfinder's Compass

You now have the Four Pillars for breakthrough communication and the I³ framework for structured discovery. But there's one more essential element: understanding your communication style and its impact on others.

Great communicators guide others toward breakthroughs. The question is: How do you become one?

Meet The Pathfinder's Compass—a tool that reveals your current communication approach and shows you the path to the most powerful style: The Pathfinder.

11

Your Transformation: Becoming a Pathfinder

Imagine someone comes to you with a problem—as a leader, sales professional, or manager.

How do you respond? What impact do you have?

The Pathfinder's Compass will show you.

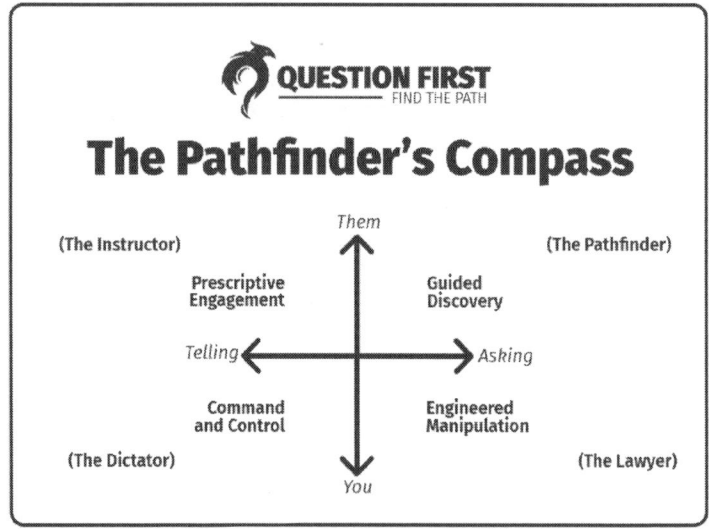

The Pathfinder's Compass

The Compass has two axes:

- **Vertical Axis:** Who benefits from the conversation? (Bottom = You, Top = Others)
- **Horizontal Axis:** Your level of curiosity (Left = Telling, Right = Asking)

This creates four distinct communication styles:

The Four Communication Styles

1. The Dictator (Self-Focused, Not Curious)

Dictators issue orders and expect compliance. They rarely ask questions, focusing solely on their own goals and what they believe is most important.

- **Sales Example:** A sales manager who says, *"You need to make 50 calls today. No excuses. Just do it."* without understanding individual challenges or circumstances.
- **Leadership Example:** A CEO who announces major changes without input: *"We're switching to this new system next month. Figure it out."*
- **Impact:** Quick results, but teams feel disempowered, creativity suffers, and long-term trust evaporates.

(Note* Dictators can be effective leaders for sure, but rarely produce a culture that develops *other* leaders along the way. And once the dictator leaves, no foundation has been left behind.)

2. The Lawyer (Self-Focused, Manipulative Curiosity)

Lawyers (in this context) ask strategic questions—appearing curious—but their real goal isn't helping their audience grow. They steer conversations toward predetermined outcomes that benefit them, using manipulation along the way.

- **Sales Example:** A rep who asks, *"You want to save money, right?"* and *"You'd agree that efficiency is important?"* leading the prospect toward their pitch rather than genuine discovery.
- **Leadership Example:** A manager who asks, *"Don't you think*

this deadline is reasonable?" when they've already decided, using questions to manipulate agreement rather than gather input.
- **Impact:** Short-term wins at the cost of long-term trust. Relationships weaken once manipulation is uncovered.

3. The Instructor (Others-Focused, Not Curious)

Instructors genuinely want to help, but they rely on *telling* rather than asking—limiting deeper understanding and growth.

- **Sales Example:** A seasoned rep who immediately jumps to solutions: *"Based on what you've told me, here's exactly what you need to do..."* without fully exploring the prospect's unique situation.
- **Leadership Example:** A well-meaning manager who says, *"Let me tell you how to handle this client situation..."* instead of helping the team member discover the solution.
- **Impact:** Effective in simple situations, but creates dependence while limiting growth, innovation, and initiative.

4. The Pathfinder (Others-Focused, Deeply Curious)

Pathfinders are the pinnacle of transformational communication. They empower others through thoughtful questions, acting as guides to create breakthrough moments.

- **Sales Example:** A rep who asks, *"Help me understand what success looks like for your team in six months. What would have to change for you to feel this project was a complete win?"*
- **Leadership Example:** A manager who guides team devel-

opment: *"What patterns do you notice in your most successful client interactions? What made those different?"*
- **Impact:** Builds deep connection while promoting engagement, innovation, and sustained success. People experience optimal growth because they're led to discover solutions themselves—not force-fed answers. And, along the way, an extraordinary, loyal, and effective team is built.

Quick Self-Assessment: What's Your Default Style?

Think about your last few important conversations—with prospects, team members, or colleagues. Be honest about your typical approach:

Reflect on these scenarios:

When someone brings you a problem (especially one you're experienced with in solving), what's your first instinct?

- Give them the solution immediately *(Instructor)*
- Ask questions to understand their situation better and help them self-discover *(Pathfinder)*
- Tell them what they need to do *(Dictator)*
- Ask leading questions to guide them to your preferred solution *(Lawyer)*

In sales conversations, do you:

- Focus solely on getting the outcome you want *(Dictator/Lawyer)*
- Genuinely seek to understand what's best for them *(Instruct

or/Pathfinder)
- Tell them what they need *(Dictator/Instructor)*
- Ask deep questions to help them discover insights *(Pathfinder)*

When someone disagrees with you, do you:

- Explain why they're wrong *(Dictator)*
- Ask questions to understand their perspective *(Pathfinder)*
- Give them more information to convince them *(Instructor)*
- Use strategic questions to change their mind *(Lawyer)*

Your goal isn't perfection—it's awareness. Once you recognize your default patterns, you can intentionally shift toward Pathfinder communication in the moments that matter most.

Your Goal: Become a Pathfinder

No one stays locked in one style. The key is self-awareness—recognizing your default approach, then intentionally shifting toward Pathfinder communication.

Your power as a communicator comes from curiosity and helping others discover their own solutions—not from controlling conversations or imposing your ideas.

If you want to be an extraordinary communicator with maximum positive influence, you must become a Pathfinder. This is the only way you and those around you will reach full potential.

The Sales Application

Here's an important nuance for sales professionals:

During Discovery: Be a full Pathfinder. Use deep curiosity, Question First, and The Law of Three to help prospects discover their real challenges through I^3.

During Recommendation: Shift to direct communication. Once I^3 is complete, give clear, authoritative recommendations: *"Here's what we recommend based on your situation."*

During Objection Handling: Return to Pathfinder mode. Use the Four Pillars to address concerns and guide toward a natural close.

The key is **intentional style shifting** based on what the conversation requires—while always maintaining your focus on the prospect's success.

The Bottom Line

Master the Four Pillars, apply I^3 systematically, and communicate as a Pathfinder. When you combine these elements, you don't just improve your sales results—you transform how you influence, lead, and connect with everyone around you.

V

Your Breakthrough Journey Starts Now

You now have the complete system: the Four Pillars, I³ Discovery Framework, and the Pathfinder's Compass. But knowledge without application is worthless.

The question isn't whether this system works—it's whether you'll do the work to make it work for you.

12

What Now?

The Most Common Mistake (And How to Avoid It)

Here's what happens to 90% of people who learn the Breakthrough System: They read this, get excited, say "Wow, we should do that," and then immediately return to their old habits the moment they get back to the office.

Don't be that person.

Transformation requires daily practice and weekly training. There are no shortcuts to mastery.

Your First 30 Days: The Foundation Phase

Daily Practice: Start every day by reviewing the Four Pillars and asking yourself:

1. **Yes, And:** What type of energy do I want to project on

today's calls?
2. **Vanguarding:** What obstacles do I need to get in front of for each conversation?
3. **Question First:** What questions will set the right tone and uncover real needs?
4. **Law of Three:** How can I create more "aha" moments with prospects today?

Weekly Training: Schedule at least one hour per week for role-playing each pillar and mastering I^3. Yes, it will feel uncomfortable at first. The Honest Agreement might seem "unnatural." That's only because you haven't practiced enough yet.

Call Analysis: Record and review your actual conversations. Where did you miss opportunities? When did you revert to old patterns?

Remember: These same practices should continue for the rest of your career. Mastery is a journey, not a destination.

Quick Win: Start a 15-minute daily huddle focused on sharpening one pillar. Small, consistent improvements compound rapidly.

What Success Looks Like

After 30 Days: You clearly understand the what, how, and why of the Four Pillars, I^3, and Pathfinder communication. You're participating in daily practice and weekly training. Your skills are clunky, but you can sense you're onto something special. You're already seeing more connection and breakthrough moments with prospects.

After 90 Days: You're really starting to "get it." You're transforming. Closing rates are up. You're creating lightbulb moments regularly. Others notice your newfound confidence and results. You're loving your job more than you have in years. You want everyone to know about the Four Pillars. The system is improving your personal communication too.

After 6 Months: Your whole life has changed. Personally and professionally, you're having better conversations than ever before. You're achieving incredible sales numbers. You have more meaningful relationships. You're riding high and excited for the future.

Implementing Organization-Wide

Start with Champions: Unless you have a small team, begin with your most influential people. Let them experience success first, then create momentum through their stories and results.

Train the Trainers: Develop internal champions who can teach others. Consider video-based certification systems for ongoing onboarding.

Include Leadership: Roll this out to your leadership team simultaneously. They need to master Pathfinder communication for their daily interactions too.

Get Expert Help: The biggest mistake is trying to do this alone. Companies that partner with The Question First Group[6] eliminate most of the learning curve and overcome resistance faster through our proven implementation process.

Overcoming Resistance

Change always creates resistance. The best way to overcome it? Proper training and early wins.

When people experience breakthrough moments in their first workshop—when they feel the power of these principles firsthand—resistance melts away and excitement takes over.

13

A Personal Story: The Power of Transformation

Chris Marr, Zach Basner, and Chris Duprey—the partners at The Question First Group (along with Marcus Sheridan)—each started in similar places. They struggled to communicate with confidence and authority. They struggled to ask the right questions and believe in their ability to lead.

But each was mentored by Marcus Sheridan, who taught them to become Pathfinders using the Four Pillars.

The transformation was dramatic. Each advanced their careers at unprecedented rates, becoming top employees, respected leaders, dynamic speakers, and gifted salespeople. They are true Pathfinders, and their energy is contagious.

The impact was so profound that they decided to create The Question First Group[7] together—to give the world the same gift they had each received.

Your Choice

You have two paths ahead of you:

Path 1: Read this, feel inspired, and return to business as usual. Keep doing what you've always done and getting what you've always gotten.

Path 2: Commit to daily practice, weekly training, and becoming a true Pathfinder. Transform not just your sales results, but your entire approach to human connection.

The choice is yours.

But remember: The world needs more Pathfinders. People who guide others to breakthrough moments. Leaders who ask powerful questions. Salespeople who create genuine connections.

Your breakthrough journey starts now.

Which path will you choose?

***

For more information on our sales workshops, coaching and training, head to questionfirstgroup.com[8] today to speak to us about the future success of your organization.

Notes

INTRODUCTION

1 Find out more about our sales workshops, training and coaching at https://questionfirstgroup.com/

IT ALL STARTS WITH...DISCOVERY

2 59% of business buyers say most sales reps don't take the time to understand them, and 73% of buyers say most sales interactions feel transactional - https://www.salesforce.com/blog/15-sales-statistics/

THE CORE PILLARS OF BREAKTHROUGH COMMUNICATION

3 If you'd like to integrate the four pillars of breakthrough communication into your organization, visit https://questionfirstgroup.com/ and schedule a session with your coach.

PILLAR I: YES, AND - THE FORCE THAT DRIVES MOMENTUM

4 The 7/38/55 Rule: https://people-shift.com/articles/mehrabians-7-38-55-communication-model/

I³: THE ROADMAP TO SUCCESS

5 Same Side Selling by Ian Altman: https://samesidesellingacademy.com/same-side-selling-book/

WHAT NOW?

6 Find out more about The Question First Group: https://questionfirstgroup.com/

A PERSONAL STORY: THE POWER OF TRANSFORMATION

7 Find out more about why we created The Question First Group: https://questionfirstgroup.com/about/

8 For more information on our sales workshops, coaching and training, head to our website today to speak to us about the future success of your organization. https://questionfirstgroup.com/

About the Author

At The Question First Group, we don't hand out answers—we help leaders and teams find their own.

We exist to transform how people communicate, lead, and solve problems by equipping them with frameworks they were never taught but desperately need. Our belief is simple: if you want to grow your business, retain great people, and create breakthrough results, it all starts with how you communicate. That means asking better questions, listening with intent, and leading with curiosity.

We've walked the path ourselves. Each of us started as strong individual contributors who struggled with confidence, communication, and leadership. But through deep mentorship, real-world application, and relentless curiosity, we became something more. Today, we're not just facilitators—we're trusted advisors to growth-minded leaders and teams who want to do their best work.

The leaders and teams we work with don't just become more effective at work—they become better partners, parents, and people. We're not here to fix anyone. We're here to help them transform into the best version of themselves.

This is not theory. It's not inspirational fluff. It's proven, practical, and personal.

You can connect with me on:
- https://questionfirstgroup.com
- https://www.linkedin.com/company/question-first

Also by The Question First Group

The 4 Pillars of Breakthrough Leadership Communication: The Pathfinder's Way

The 4 Pillars of Breakthrough Client Communication: The Pathfinder's Way

Made in the USA
Middletown, DE
25 November 2025